Whose Tools Are These?

A Look at Tools Workers Use—
Big, Sharp, and Smooth

by Sharon Katz Cooper
illustrated by Amy Bailey Muehlenhardt

PICTURE WINDOW BOOKS
Minneapolis, Minnesota

Special thanks to our advisers for their expertise:

Rick Levine, Publisher
Made To Measure and Uniform Market News Magazine
Highland Park, Illinois

Susan Kesselring, M.A., Literacy Educator
Rosemount–Apple Valley–Eagan (Minnesota) School District

Editor: Christianne Jones
Designer: Joe Anderson
Page Production: Amy Bailey Muehlenhardt
Editorial Director: Carol Jones
Creative Director: Keith Griffin
The illustrations in this book were created digitally.

Picture Window Books
1710 Roe Crest Drive
North Mankato, MN 56003
www.capstonepub.com

Library of Congress Cataloging-in-Publication Data
Cooper, Sharon Katz.
Whose tools are these? : a look at tools workers use—big, sharp, and smooth / by Sharon Katz Cooper ;
illustrated by Amy Bailey Muehlenhardt.
p. cm. — (Whose is it?)
Includes bibliographical references and index.
ISBN-13: 978-1-4048-1602-2 (hardcover)
ISBN-13: 978-1-4048-1978-8 (paperback)
1. Tools—Juvenile literature. I. Muehlenhardt, Amy Bailey, 1974- ill. II. Title. III. Series.

GN436.8C66 2006
621.9—dc22   2005021852

Use your thinking tool and guess whose tools are whose.

Tools can be big, small, soft, hard, sharp, or smooth. A fork is a tool to help you eat. A shovel is a tool to help you dig. Many people use tools to cook, clean, and fix things.

Many workers use special tools to do their jobs. Can you tell whose tools are whose?

Look in the back for more information about tools.

Whose tools are these,
looking and listening?

These are a doctor's tools.

She uses them to peek in your ears, shine light in your eyes, or listen to your heart. A doctor's tools help her see if you are healthy. If you are sick, she can use her tools to find out why. Then she can help you get better.

Fun Fact: Doctors get help from other people and tools. Radiology technicians use X-ray machines to take a picture of your insides. A doctor looks at the X-ray pictures to see what's going on inside your body.

Whose tools are these,
so shiny and sharp?

These are a chef's tools.

A chef needs different kinds of tools to prepare different types of foods. He has tools for cutting and tools for measuring. He has other tools for mixing, chopping, and blending.

Fun Fact: You may have some of the same tools a chef uses. Which tools do you use to help cook dinner or bake cookies?

Whose tool is this, making far away objects look closer?

9

This is a field biologist's tool.

A biologist is a kind of scientist. She observes animals to learn what they do. A biologist wants to sit far from the animals so she doesn't scare them. She needs binoculars to help her see what the animals are doing.

Fun Fact: Binoculars magnify objects that are far away. A magnifying glass works the same way to make tiny objects look bigger. You might use a magnifying glass to look at tiny insects on a sidewalk.

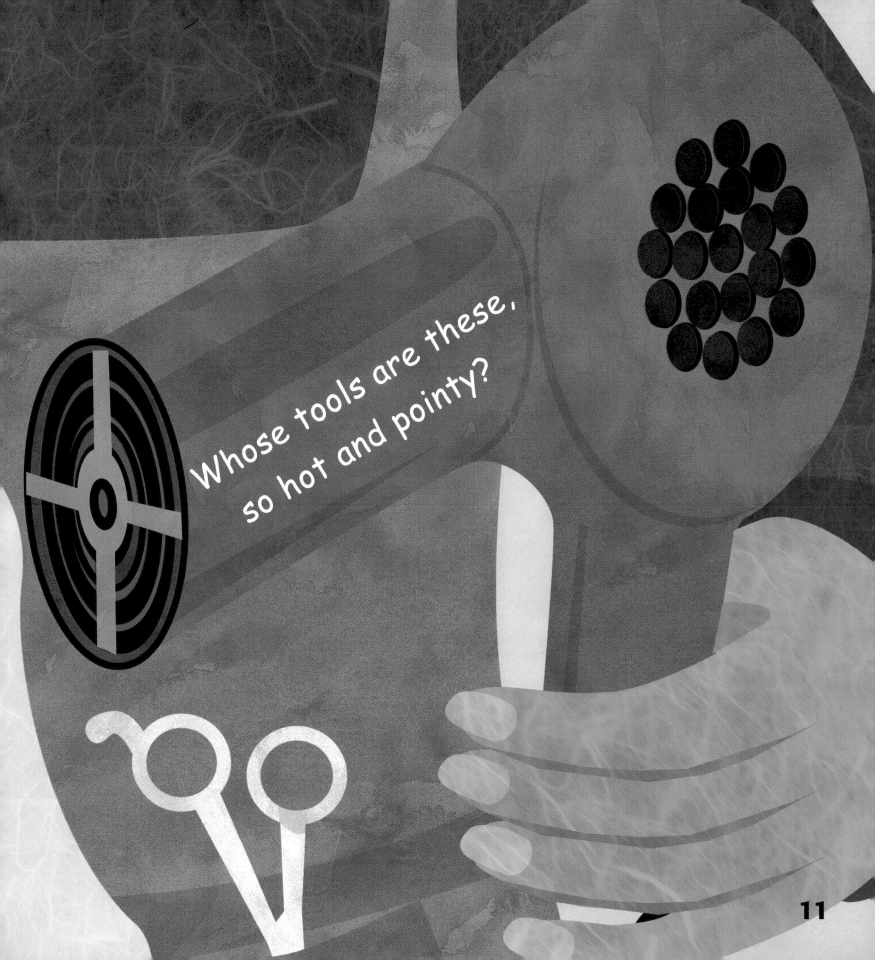

These are a hairdresser's tools.

She uses a blow dryer to dry hair, a comb or brush to style hair, and a scissors to cut hair. She might use a clip to keep hair in place and a hot curling iron to curl hair.

Fun Fact: A hairdresser can change the way a person looks. She can use her tools to straighten hair if it is curly. She can also curl hair if it is straight. She can even change the color of hair.

Whose tools are these, sitting on a desk?

These are a teacher's tools.

A teacher helps children learn.
He uses dry erase markers to write
numbers and words on the board.
He shares books with his class to help
children learn to read. He might show
a video to teach about a far away place.

A B C D E F G H

$$5$$
$$+\ 5$$
$$10$$

Fun Fact: A teacher can use almost anything as a tool.
He might teach math with a pizza. He might teach
science with a ball. Do your teachers use more than
one tool?

Whose tools are these, so colorful and bright?

These are an artist's tools.

She uses colors and brushes to paint a picture. She uses a drawing table to hold her paints and her canvas. Some painters also paint houses and walls. They use much larger brushes and many other tools like ladders and sprayers.

Fun Fact: Paint brushes have bristles. Bristles can be stiff or soft. They can be made from the hair of squirrels, hogs, oxen, ponies, goats, or other man-made materials.

These are a lifeguard's tools.

At a beach or pool, a lifeguard keeps people safe. Sometimes a lifeguard needs to stop people from pushing or running. He might blow his whistle to get their attention. He uses a rescue tube to bring a person out of the water if the person has trouble swimming.

Fun Fact: People use their arms and legs as tools for swimming. Animals that live in water have even better tools for swimming. Fish use fins. Frogs use webbed feet.

Whose tools are these,
so helpful and varied?

These are your tools!

You need your pencil and a good eraser to do your homework. If you are doing math, you might need a ruler. If you are doing art, you might need markers, paint, or crayons. If you are writing a story, you might need a dictionary. Whatever subject you are working on, you have to use your most important tool—your brain!

Fun Fact: When your brain is fully developed, it will weight about 3 pounds (1.35 kilograms).

Just for Fun

Whose tool is whose? Point to the picture
of the tool described in each sentence.

* I help make people look their best.

hairdresser's tools

* I help make delicious meals.

chef's tools

* My bristles can be stiff or soft.

artist's tools

All About Tools

Tools on the Go

Doctors used to visit the patients' homes. They would bring all their tools with them in a big black bag.

Tool Size

Tools come in all sizes. Some are tiny and others are quite large. Have you ever seen a tiny screwdriver or a huge crane? These are both tools people use to do their jobs.

Animal Tools

Even animals use tools. Field biologists have watched chimpanzees and orangutans use sticks to dig. These sticks help them find insects or worms to eat.

Technology Tools

Today, a lot of tools are electronic. Workers in many jobs use computers. Computers come in all sizes and do many different tasks. Cell phones, printers, and fax machines are all important tools, too.

Glossary

binoculars–a tool that makes far-away objects look closer

bristles–hair-like objects on the end of a paint brush

canvas–a piece of cloth on a frame that is used as a painting surface

magnify–to make something look larger

webbed feet–feet with wide flaps of skin between the toes

X-ray–a picture taken of the inside of the body that can show if something is wrong

X-ray machine–a piece of equipment that uses very fast beams of light that you can't see to take a picture of something inside a person's body

To Learn More

At the Library

Kelley, True. *Hammers and Mops, Pencils, and Pots: A First Book of Tools and Gadgets We Use around the House*. New York: Crown, 1994.

Morris, Ann. *Tools*. New York: Mulberry Books, 1998.

Snyder, Inez. *School Tools*. New York: Children's Press, 2002.

On the Web

FactHound offers a safe, fun way to find Internet sites related to this book. All of the sites on FactHound have been researched by our staff.

1. Visit *www.facthound.com*
2. Type in this special code for age-appropriate sites: 140481602X
3. Click on the FETCH IT button.

Your trusty FactHound will fetch the best sites for you!

Index

Look for all of the books in the Whose Is It? series:

Whose Coat Is This?
1-4048-1598-8

Whose Ears Are These?
1-4048-0004-2

Whose Eyes Are These?
1-4048-0005-0

Whose Feet Are These?
1-4048-0006-9

Whose Food Is This?
1-4048-0607-5

Whose Gloves Are These?
1-4048-1599-6

Whose Hat Is This?
1-4048-1600-3

Whose House Is This?
1-4048-0608-3

Whose Legs Are These?
1-4048-0007-7

Whose Mouth Is This?
1-4048-0008-5

Whose Nose Is This?
1-4048-0009-3

Whose Shadow Is This?
1-4048-0609-1

Whose Shoes Are These?
1-4048-1601-1

Whose Skin Is This?
1-4048-0010-7

Whose Sound Is This?
1-4048-0610-5

Whose Spots Are These?
1-4048-0611-3

Whose Tail Is This?
1-4048-0011-5

Whose Tools Are These?
1-4048-1602-X

Whose Vehicle Is This?
1-4048-1603-8

Whose Work Is This?
1-4048-0612-1